Harnett Lane

Joshua Merten

Harnett Lane

Dedicated to Hannah and Grampy's garden

The most heartfelt thanks to Anthony Skuse for your guidance and giving imagination, Reuben Solomon and the Writers' Group at Actors Centre Australia for the beautiful space you foster, and my sister Elise for twenty years alongside you.

This collection was pieced together in Gadigal, Wangal and Kuringai Country. Aboriginal and Torres Strait Islander peoples are the first storytellers of these lands. Sovereignty was never ceded.

Harnett Lane
ISBN 978 1 76109 636 5
Copyright © text Joshua Merten 2023
Cover image: Elise Merten

First published 2023 by
GINNINDERRA PRESS
PO Box 3461 Port Adelaide 5015
www.ginninderrapress.com.au

Contents

回家 (huí jiā) – I	7
回家 – II	8
World of Ordinary People	9
Grey Day	10
Cardboard Skin	11
Punch-drunk	12
Maroubra	13
Harnett Lane	14
Railway Street	15
Moments in Wynyard	16
Crave	17
Fishnets	18
Fast-forward	19
Circular Quay	20
Turnover	21
回家 – III	22
21 Vernon Street	23
Cedarwood	24
Three Poems – Rats	25
Delay	26
A Little Tune	27
Smoky Bedroom	28
Morgan Street	29
Half-asleep at Burwood	30
Bees	31
Sleeping Streets	32
In-between Things	33

'The meaning? Look, it's snowing.'
— Anton Chekhov, *Three Sisters*

回家 (huí jiā) – I

The clouds glazing across
Graphite grey faces and
Cracked hands
Brush the grassy rubble on

Kowloon Peak as
Red duck skins glisten in
Yellow lights and

Smoke from a thousand cigarettes
Cradled by fingertips
Fills the wrinkles under tin roofs.

A fur hat and
A smoking pipe say,
Under the fizz of expired firecrackers,
'孩子要乖，少出声.'
Children should be seen, not heard.

He shuffles on his pillow
And runs his tongue between his teeth.

回家 – II

The uneven ground
At Jankrik bus stop
Curves like skin over broken bones and
Two oversized button-ups
Squatting on a cracked stair
Share a cigarette while
Rusted barrels of burnt rubbish
Roll amalgamated smells
Into the crumbled road.

Plates of ayam goreng
Taste half-sweet,
And bamboo stalks
Grow across each other
Like stitching.

World of Ordinary People

In this world
Of ordinary people
A lamp brightens an
Empty dress shop
A highway is redressed
As alleys fester

Flash cars sit
Engineless
In a window,
The gym wall turns green
Skin sweats and burns lean
Under fluorescents

A second cigarette
Partners lips and fingertips
Under humming neon bars,
Three toothy muzzles
Chuck syllables
At passers-by
Piss stinks in patches
Of pears and sourness.

When it rains
In this world
Of ordinary people
It feels like
It's raining everywhere.

Grey Day

Everything is greyer than usual
And I am compensating
By trying to convince myself
That life still is interesting,
Still is surprising,
And that I am right to be curious about it.

Driving home from the grocery store
After buying spaghetti
Tinned tomatoes
Beef mince
Butter,
I saw my ex-girlfriend
After nearly a month without talking.
We agreed to have coffee
When I pick up my surfboard from her house.
I miss her parents.

At my window
I opened my phone
And wrote a poem
Between domestic tasks.
I like how the kettle sings to me.
I sip my tea.

Cardboard Skin

On rainy days
When eyelids fold in and
Thread themselves closed

With odes and odours of
Concrete roads
Carve me into the shelf with

The hand-me-downs
And the sand
Trapped in thongs and

Wash my cardboard skin
In saltwater silhouettes.

Punch-drunk

We drown ourselves in hymns and lyrics
Spirits and simple syrups
To sneak up on ourselves
In shared silences,

To trace skin in watercolours
And paint necks in muted hues
Of imagined things.

Lips split like riptides as minds swim away
And swelling waves sweep
Heels and heads in circles
Cracking skulls on seabeds
And steps in saxophone licks
In Pyrmont bars

While fingertips impressing arm hairs
Tickle that twitching itch,
That punch-drunk desire to fix and be fixed.

Maroubra

The ice in the white water and
The crystal specks in the wind
Melt under summer sun as
Sand clasps pointed toes
Taps shower ankles
The sun crawls across Atlas's back
Waves wander the point
And clouds watch the rock face crack.
The sea hugs his limbs like tattoo sleeves.

Harnett Lane

Crisp Sydney air in autumn
Tapping chapped lips
And freshly wet hair
Bends memory around
That downhill driveway
Back to Bowral.

Pink paint licks fingertips
Tadpoles quiver in the bird bath

A screw sleeps on a workbench
In a shed with a million tools

And a daddy long legs lounges
In the windowsill.

The picture frames and
Silk curtains
Sap to a chapel white

Mossy logs settle
The stone fireplace.

The garden
Dangles into bush and
Pink and purple flowers mesh
Into each other's edges

Melting out from this house
Where bedhead patterns tattoo skin
And memories fold themselves in.

Railway Street

A dew-pecked dandelion tickles
Its fresh spine
Against the rusted fence

An empty Coopers can
Settles the soil on
The edges of Railway Street

The wind traces concrete
Scarred skin clasped
Sunshine hums through the peepholes on
Hollow station steps

A black cat
Curls its back against the graffiti
And licks her fur.

Moments in Wynyard

A jacaranda flower
Crisp on cement.
Thirty black shoes step around.
You only hurt the ones you love
Lyrics muffled
Through a damp beard.
A couple argue
Rope–burn on palms,
Thirty black shoes step around.
'Just thought I'd tell you something funny.
I feel bigger here, not smaller.'

Crave

Goodbyes beside windows
Silhouetted bare branches like
A hundred fingers crossed
Gentle twitches
Skin over her ribs.

The song plays over.
So here I am.

CRAVE sprayed on a no-stopping sign.

Fishnets

Purple twilight sticks to skin
Like leather stitching
LEDs stain the cracked glass windows

A pair of hazel eyes
And crow-black heels
Taps cigarette butts out

On the split concrete
Rust-red hair
Softens over his nape

Like glistening candle wax
And fishnet stockings clutch his thighs
As he marches on

In search of tongues
To lick his wounds.

Fast-forward

Rearranging furniture
For an audience
That never arrives –

Put it back where it was
Before.

Fast-forward
Heaped sugar spoons
Firecrackers flacking
Fingertips on skin
Pupils pool inward
Sailboats untied from piers
Passing over ocean trenches

Fall in.
Fast-forward
Click life away
Staring screens squint into square retinas
Melting into empty thumbs.

Fast-forward
Episode after episode
That person and that person
Left,

Left

Left.

Circular Quay

Honey-hued sunlight hovers
Over arm hairs as
A wet beard cradles a cold meal.

A million washed hands meet
In a million windows
While rooftop gardens cap cracked doorsteps.

On lamplit station bridges
Stiff calves and sore blisters let
Tired words slip after

Loose kisses and
Expired lipstick spills
Over old wishlists.

Turnover

A folded coffee cup rests
On concrete, fondled
By the stretching fluorescents
Of automatic doors

Graffiti licks the stop sign
While the bar-side switch flicks
And confetti flakes
From scaffolded ceilings.

The piano shop waits
For the bus schedule to turn over
As the street lamp traps
A rainy halo over
The idle row of tin roofs,
Cold hands flatten on the mattress.

Between the hum
And the screech
The palm and the plastic
Lies the day.

Leathered steps click over
The handprint in the concrete,
Past pastel puffer jackets
And the blue plastic bag attached to the pram.
The wrinkled curtains
Fold over the Polish café
And the yellow fumes
Tap tinted windows.

回家 – III

The sky sheds
A gentle coat
Of salt specks tickling
The Warriewood headland,
Brushing the concrete.

My cigarette
Flakes away
Like mandarin peels
Along the silky canvas.

The jacarandas change colour in the heat.

21 Vernon Street

Eyelashes close under
Crepe myrtle leaves,
A nose-length away.

The cocker spaniel that
Barks at night
Trots out to play.
Flopping thongs waddle behind,
Hand on wrist
Bobbing with the concrete.

Newborn baby
Please knock
Do not use doorbell
Thanks.

Hot winds massage the trees.

Cedarwood

Drowsy candlewax wraps
The corner of
The cedarwood coffee table
And cream cotton towels
Stacked in threes
Soften into each other
As peanut oil and beef marinade
Fog the ceramic tiles
On the little kitchen wall.
My hair drips salt
And my nose runs,
The curled seashell light in my hands,
My hands heavy on the table.

Three Poems – Rats

The black puffer jacket
Hushes against itself,
Purple nail polish
Tapping his jaw.

Fifty eager pigeons pick
At the shopfront,
Weaving like rats.

Aircon blades whirr –
Attached like ticks
To the apartment block back.

Delay

Seven forty-four.
My hair falls out in the shower
With the glitter.
Junk mail scatters the damp footpath
Bleeding into bin juice
Bird shit on the windshield and
Soggy leaves stuck in tyre holes.
I pocket my hands.
Seven fifty-six Schofield via Parramatta
A kid touches a dead pigeon
Black laces tied too tight—
Doors closing
Pink gum licks the train seat
As suitcase wheels twitch with the train's squeaks
And leftover headspins.

A Little Tune

And in the silence I hummed a little tune.
Do you remember?

Filthy sleeves,
The sour taste of sick.

Familiar movements on different skin
And Brighton Street.

A rusty green fence
And a rusty green roof.

A layer of jacaranda flowers
On the platform,
Twitching.

And in the silence I hummed a little tune.

Smoky Bedroom

He smoked
A cigarette
For the third time yesterday.
It tasted of
Strangers' lips
And stone fruits.
Opening the window
Didn't let enough smoke escape,
So he'll wait till morning
For fresh air.

Morgan Street

Christmas presents in plastic bags and
Two half-drunk shiraz bottles
Purple Converse flap
Dirty laces on the street
Windy streets smell of campfires
Marble-cold lips
Fold over like
The fluorescents at my letter box
The cockroach in the cupboard.

Half-asleep at Burwood

Stretching station lamps swallow
Studio apartments laced in
Sweaty yellow glows
And shallow sighs.

Waving from the platform
A weathered sandstone beard
Nearly three dollars in a coffee cup.
Trains creep in slow like millipedes

Rest.
Pass, heaving.

Sparks crack against iron beams
While a hundred tight-laced feet
Rest purpling bruises.

Bees

Humming into a croaking throat
Pulling painted nails up to parted lips

The roads sing to the rooftops in
Muffled moans.

Three bees twitch together
Pollen-drunk wings flick in wind

Buzzing brass harmonies
Coat tired eyes in nicotine.

Sleeping Streets

Six empty buses shuffle across Oxford Street
Dress shops bleed neon
As no-stopping signs lean

Like cicadas to bonfires
And hours spread themselves over skin
Mist bathes the road

Drunk eyelids on
Bus windows
Purr against the glass
Over the sleeping street.

In-between Things

He likes the things in-between definitions
They remind him that things existed
Before we started letting them.
This morning
He apologised to a tree
For avoiding her,
He spent four dollars
That changed his day
And said 'good luck' to a stranger,
He missed someone
He'd wanted gone.
The in-between things are kind
Their edges aren't sharp
They sing to the ordinary.

www.ingramcontent.com/pod-product-compliance
Lightning Source LLC
Chambersburg PA
CBHW071509080526
44587CB00016B/2733